VAN GOGH'S PROVENCE

THE SOWER, JUNE 1888

VAN GOGH'S
PROVENCE

TIGER BOOKS INTERNATIONAL

TOULOUSE-LAUTREC'S PASTEL *PORTRAIT OF VINCENT VAN GOGH*, 1887

INTRODUCTION

In the autumn of 1886, Vincent van Gogh, living at the time in Paris, wrote to the English painter Horace Livens, telling him, 'I may be going to the South of France, the land of the blue tones and bright colours'.

His dream of going south had a number of motives. Vincent (1853-90) and his younger brother Theo (1857-91), an art dealer, were both admirers of Adolphe Monticelli, a Provençal painter, and of Paul Cézanne who worked in Provence. Vincent had met the leading Impressionists, including Camille Pissarro, who encouraged him to consider the advantages of painting in the South of France. He wanted to travel to a land where the light and colours were bright, as he later described his aspiration to Theo, '... wishing to see a different light, thinking that looking at nature under a bright sky might give us a better idea of the Japanese way of feeling and drawing.' Of these bright, hard-edged Japanese landscapes he later wrote to Paul Gauguin, '... there is still present in my mind the emotion produced by my own journey from Paris to Arles last winter. How I peered out to see if it was like Japan yet! Childish, wasn't it?' Paul Gauguin figured in his vague plan to establish a 'Studio of the South', where fellow artists could live and work together. Vincent was familiar with the Provençal novels of Emile Zola and Alphonse Daudet, especially the latter's *Tartarin de Tarascon* (1872), from which he often quoted. And finally, he hoped to improve his health after two years of dissipation in Paris.

His decision came after the failure of his earlier careers as an art dealer and then a missionary. Now, with no other means of financial support, he was entirely dependent on Theo. Much of what we know of Vincent's two-year stay in Provence comes from his letters to Theo, to his youngest sister, Wilhelmina

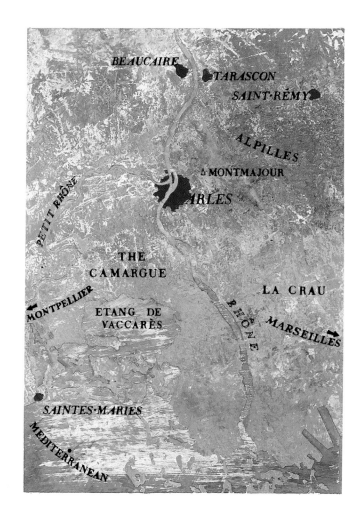

Jacoba van Gogh (known as 'Wil') and to other relatives and fellow artists. Originally edited by Theo's wife Johanna van Gogh, née Bonger, they are among the most revealing in the history of art. Not only did they enable him to collect and convey his thoughts about art in general and his paintings and drawings in particular, but they served to relieve his loneliness and acted as a verbal record, just as his paintings provide us with a visual record of his stay in Provence.

No one knows why Vincent specifically chose Arles, a Roman city founded by Julius Caesar and a port some 25 miles from the estuary of the Rhône. Degas and other artist friends had visited the town, whose female inhabitants were famed for their beauty, and may have persuaded him of its attractions. Although Arles was off the tourist track, industry came to it in the mid-nineteenth century with the building of the railway. Vincent stepped from the Paris train in Arles on 22 February 1888, and was astonished to find that two feet of snow lay on the ground. He took a room at the Hôtel-Restaurant Carrel. The day after his arrival he wrote to Theo, 'Here in Arles the country seems flat. I have seen some splendid red stretches of soil planted with vines. And the landscapes in the snow, with the summits white against a sky as luminous as the snow, were just like the winter landscapes that the Japanese have painted.' He later informed Theo, 'I am still convinced that nature down here is just what one wants to provide colour. So that it's more than likely I shall hardly ever budge from here.'

The more he explored the Provençal landscape, the more excited Vincent became. After the drab north of his native Holland, and Belgium and Paris where he had been working, 'the different light' he was seeking and the beautiful countryside presented a wealth of possible subjects. Not long after his arrival he wrote to the painter Emile Bernard, '. . . this country seems as beautiful as Japan as far as the limpidity of the atmosphere and the brilliant colour effects are concerned. Water forms patches of a beautiful emerald or a rich blue in the landscape . . . the sunsets have a pale orange colour which makes the fields appear blue.' He told Theo, 'Nature here is so *extraordinarily* beautiful. Everywhere and all over the vault of heaven is marvellous blue, and the sun sheds a radiance of pure sulphur, and it is soft and lovely as the combination of heavenly blues and yellows in a Van der Meer of Delft.'

Far from hurtling at random into his work, as is often implied,

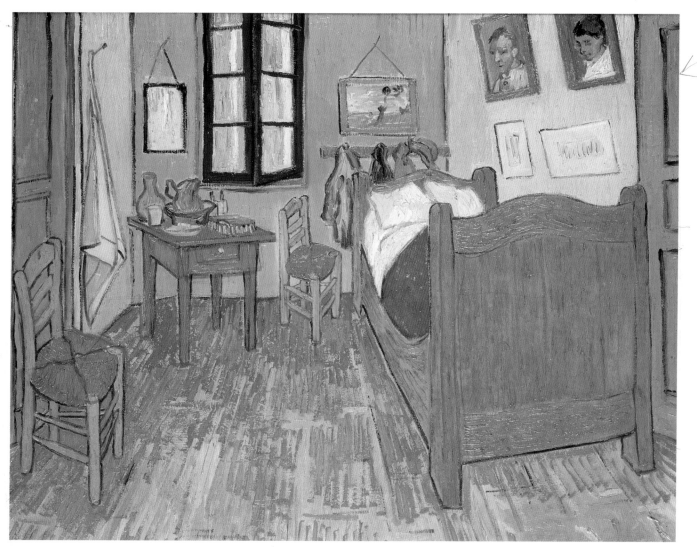

Vincent's Room in Arles, a replica painted at Saint-Remy

LEFT: *L'ARLÉSIENNE*, ONE OF VINCENT'S PORTRAITS OF MADAME GINOUX
RIGHT: *DR FÉLIX REY*, VINCENT'S DOCTOR AT ARLES, JANUARY 1889

Vincent approached his new environment in a meticulous fashion, undertaking long walks in his search for suitable motifs, carefully planning his compositions, which often took him back to the same locations time and time again, to paint or draw several versions of the same subject. 'To get at the real character of things here, you must look at them and paint them for a long time,' he explained to Theo. His favourite sites included the Rhône quays and bridges, the ruined abbey of Montmajour, the plain known as La Crau, local fields and orchards, and his own house and the neighbouring park. He also made several short excursions to places further afield, including Saintes-Maries on the coast. Although he featured the Roman ruins known as Les Alyscamps, he was generally less interested in the tourists' Provence than in the Provence of the Provençals and all that nature offered in this sunny landscape.

In the course of his stay in the region, Vincent completely revolutionized his style, discarding his practice of producing a preliminary drawing (although he often drew copies to send to Theo and others, sometimes using the Japanese device of a reed pen), and began applying paint directly to his canvas, perhaps squeezed directly from tubes – which were a fairly new invention. His speed of working thus increased, and during his relatively brief stay of 444 days in Arles – some of it unproductive as a result of his hospitalization – he produced some 200 paintings and over 100 drawings. On occasions he worked at a feverish rate – in June 1888, for example, he executed ten paintings of harvest scenes in as many days.

In an attempt to establish his Studio of the South, Vincent invited Paul Gauguin to stay. Part of his motive must also have been to relieve his isolation, and he certainly felt that the two of

INTERIOR OF THE HOSPITAL AT ARLES, LATER COMPLETED AT SAINT-RÉMY

them could live as cheaply as one – though in fact Theo was also supporting Gauguin through a commitment to buy twelve paintings a year, sending him a monthly allowance. Before his arrival on 23 October 1888, Vincent wrote to him, 'It is beginning to turn cold, particularly in the days when the mistral blows. I have had gas laid on in the studio, so that we shall have good light in winter. Perhaps Arles will disappoint you, if you come here in mistral weather; but you wait – it is only in the long run that the poetry of this place penetrates.'

Gauguin joined Vincent in painting a number of local scenes and both painted Arlésiennes, local women in traditional costume, including portraits of two women of Vincent's acquaintance, Madame Ginoux the innkeeper's wife and Madame Roulin the postman's wife. Gauguin also painted Vincent at work painting sunflowers.

Almost immediately, however, Gauguin was highly critical of his new environment, even causing Vincent to begin to have doubts about the advantages of Provence over those of Gauguin's favoured territory of Brittany. A series of arguments ensued and Gauguin announced his decision to return to Paris, but quickly changed his mind. Their rows culminated in the incident of Vincent's lopping off part of his left ear. Just two months after Gauguin took up residence in Vincent's 'Yellow House', on Sunday 23 December, according to Gauguin's later explanation, Vincent threatened him with razor and as a result, in fear of his life, he went to a local hotel for the night. Vincent

THE GARDEN OF ST PAUL'S HOSPITAL IN SAINT-REMY, OCTOBER 1889

returned to the Yellow House and mutilated himself. Gauguin quietly left Arles, never to return, while Vincent was taken to hospital. Years later, Gauguin justified his part in the event, claiming that Vincent was mad, but it seems likely that the dramatic episode occurred after a period of great tension that arose when the two artists were compelled to remain indoors during several days of unusually heavy rain, and major differences of opinion had arisen. The circumstances, like the actual causes of Vincent's 'madness', which have been attributed to an ear disorder known as Ménières disease, as well as to everything from absinthe poisoning, epilepsy and schizophrenia to syphilis, remain a subject of fascinating speculation.

Vincent stayed at Arles hospital for two weeks, where he was visited by his friend the postman Joseph Roulin who took him home, but a month later he was back in hospital suffering from the delusion that he was being poisoned. After his discharge he began to seek explanations for his own behaviour and put it down to the climate, drinking, his unbalanced diet and excessive smoking. A group of locals was less detached, however, and he was presented with a petition signed by 29 Arlésiens demanding he be returned to the care of his family or preferably be installed in a mental asylum. He duly returned to the hospital under a police escort, and while there was visited by the painter Paul Signac. During this period he recovered sufficiently to execute several paintings of the hospital interior and gardens and, gradually, the surrounding countryside.

Vincent's stay at Arles was followed by his move to the asylum of Saint-Paul-de-Mausole at Saint-Rémy as a voluntary inmate. The asylum, a former Augustinian monastery about two miles outside the town, lay 15 miles to the north-east of Arles, with the Alpilles mountains to the south. It was surrounded by walled gardens and fields which Vincent could see from his room. During his year-long stay there, Vincent was to produce such memorable works as *Irises*, painted within the hospital grounds, as well as his famed paintings of cypresses and wheatfields. On several excursions into the mountains he depicted something of the more rugged Provençal landscape. He eventually decided to leave Provence and thought of staying with Camille Pissarro at Eragny, but he in turn suggested that Vincent should seek help from Dr Paul Gachet of Auvers-sur-Oise, an amateur artist and doctor. It was during his stay there that he committed suicide.

On 14 May 1890, just before his departure for Paris to visit Theo, prior to his move to Auvers, Vincent wrote to his brother, 'I saw the country again after the rain, quite fresh and full of flowers – what things I could still have done.'

THE PLATES

MOUNTAIN LANDSCAPE SEEN ACROSS THE WALLS, APRIL 1890

DRAWBRIDGE WITH CARRIAGE (LE PONT DE LANGLOIS)
March 1888
State Museum Kröller-Müller, Otterlo

'I brought back a size 15 [25½ × 19¾ inches / 65 × 50 cm] canvas today. It is a drawbridge with a little cart going over it, outlined against a blue sky – the river blue as well, the banks orange coloured with green grass and a group of women washing linen wearing smocks and multicoloured caps.'

Letter to Theo

The bridge known as the Pont de Langlois (after a bridge-keeper of that name, but misheard by Vincent as 'Pont de l'Anglais') crossed the canal built in the early nineteenth century, on the south side of Arles at Port-de-Bouc. Harking back to the bridges he knew at home in Holland, this bright, sunny painting is regarded as Vincent's first notable work of his Arles period, and has remained among his most popular and widely reproduced subjects. It is known that he was very satisfied with it and regarded it as one of his most successful compositions, executing several subtly different versions of it.

ORCHARD IN BLOOM
March 1888
National Gallery of Scotland, Edinburgh

'I'm up to my ears in work, for the trees are in blossom and I want to paint a Provençal orchard of astounding gaiety.'

'I have another orchard, as good as the pink peach trees, apricot trees of a very pale pink. At the moment I am working on some plum trees, yellowish-white, with thousands of black branches ... You know I am changeable in my work, and this craze for painting orchards will not last for ever.'

Letters to Theo

'I don't regret having come here, for I think the scenery here extremely beautiful . . . . I am working on six paintings of fruit trees in bloom.'

Letter to Wilhelmina van Gogh

'At the moment I am absorbed in the blossoming fruit trees, pink peach trees and yellow-white pear trees. My brush stroke has no system at all. I hit the canvas with irregular touches of the brush, which I leave as they are. Patches of thickly laid-on colour, spots of canvas left uncovered, here and there portions that are left absolutely unfinished, repetitions, savageries.'

Letter to Emile Bernard

Vincent spent several weeks painting his new subject of orchards in what he described as 'a frenzy of work'. During a period of three weeks, while the blossom was at its peak, he painted more than ten works.

Harvest Landscape

June 1888

Vincent van Gogh Foundation/National Museum Vincent van Gogh, Amsterdam

'I keep on finding very beautiful and interesting subjects here.'

'I am working on a landscape with wheatfields.'

'[Provence] has become very different from what it was in spring, and yet I have certainly no less love for this countryside, scorched as it begins to be from now on. Everywhere now there is old gold, bronze, copper, one might say, and this with the green azure of the sky blanched with heat: a delicious colour, extraordinarily harmonious, with the blended tones of Delacroix.'

'I am working on a new subject, fields green and yellow as far as the eye can see. I have already drawn it twice, and I am starting it again as a painting.'

'. . . it isn't at all finished, but it kills everything else I have done.'

Letters to Theo

Considered one of the great masterpieces of Vincent's Arles period, this magnificent panoramic view of the Provençal landscape contains one of his depictions of the ruins of Montmajour, seen in the distance on the left.

VIEW OF SAINTES-MARIES
June 1888
State Museum Kröller-Müller, Otterlo

'I brought three canvases and have covered them – two seascapes, a view of the village, and then some drawings which I will send you by post, when I return tomorrow to Arles . . . . I do not think there are a hundred houses in the village, or town. The chief building after the old church, and an ancient fortress, is the barracks. And the houses – like the ones on our heaths and peat-bogs in Drenthe; you will see some specimens of them in the drawings.'

Letter to Theo

In early June 1888 Vincent went to Saintes-Maries-de-la-Mer, a little fishing village not far from Arles. His painting of the fortified village church and surrounding cottages was his only general view of Saintes-Maries, but he also produced a number of paintings based on the drawings of the cottages to which he refers in his letter.

FISHING BOATS ON THE BEACH
June 1888
Vincent van Gogh Foundation/National Museum Vincent van Gogh, Amsterdam

'At last I have seen the Mediterranean .... I have spent a week at Saintes-Maries, and to get there drove in a stagecoach across the Camargue with its vineyards, moors and flat fields like Holland .... On the perfectly flat, sandy beach little boats, green, red, blue boats, so pretty in shape and colour that they made one think of flowers.'

Letter to Emile Bernard

The flat landscape of southern Provence often reminded Vincent of his homeland. He made a drawing of the boats just before he left, with copious colour notes, and painted it on his return to Arles. He was impressed with his increased output, telling Theo, 'I have only been here a few months, but tell me this – could I, in Paris, have done the drawing of the boats *in an hour*?'

CARAVANS
August 1888
Musée d'Orsay, Paris

The subject of a gipsy encampment with caravans and horses, described to Theo as '. . . a little study of a roadside inn, with red and green carts', is unique in Vincent's work, but its theme is typically simple and unpretentious. Also known as *Les Bohémiens*, or gipsies, he encountered them by chance on the road to Saintes-Maries, to which they traditionally travelled every year to attend the local horse fair. Vincent enjoyed the company of aliens and social outsiders, such as the Zouaves, the Algerian troops stationed in Arles, whom he also painted, and undoubtedly appreciated the freedom and proximity to nature implied by the Romany lifestyle.

SUNFLOWERS
August 1888
Bayerische Staatsgemäldesammlungen,
Neue Pinakothek, Munich

SUNFLOWERS
August 1888
National Gallery, London

'I am thinking of decorating my studio with half-a-dozen pictures of sunflowers, a decoration in which the raw or broken chrome yellows will blaze forth on various backgrounds – blue, from the palest malachite green to royal blue, framed in thin strips of wood painted with orange lead. Effects like those of stained-glass windows in a Gothic church.'

Letter to Emile Bernard

Vincent told his brother that he was inspired to paint sunflowers after seeing them in the window of the restaurant next to Theo's Paris gallery, describing them as 'a symphony in blue and yellow'. He told him, 'I am working at it every morning from sunrise on, for the flowers wilt so quickly and it is a matter of doing the whole thing in one go.'

THE NIGHT CAFÉ
September 1888
Yale University Art Gallery, New Haven, Connecticut

'Today I am probably going to start on the interior of the café where I eat, by gaslight, in the evening. It is what they call here a "café de nuit" (they are fairly common here), staying open all night.'

Letter to Theo

'I have just finished a canvas representing the interior of a night café lighted with lamps. A number of poor night wanderers are asleep in a corner. The room is painted red, and in it, under the gaslight, a green billiard table casts an immense shadow on the boarded floor. There are six or seven reds in this canvas, from blood red to delicate pink, contrasting with as many pale or deep greens.'

Letter to Wilhelmina van Gogh

During the early months of his stay in Arles, Vincent rented a room in the Café de la Gare, run by Joseph and Marie Ginoux, whom he painted on several occasions. It was close to his Yellow House, which he used only as a studio before making it habitable. He told Theo he had 'Stayed up three nights to paint it, while sleeping during the day.' Gauguin painted his own version of the café interior, placing Mme Ginoux in the foreground. Vincent wrote to his sister Wilhelmina, 'In my painting *The Night Café* I have tried to express the idea that the café is a place where a person can ruin himself, go mad, commit crimes.'

CAFÉ TERRACE AT NIGHT
September 1888
State Museum Kröller-Müller, Otterlo

'. . . a new picture representing the outside of a night café. On the terrace are tiny figures of people drinking. An enormous yellow lantern sheds its light on the terrace, the façade, the pavement, and even casts a light on the paving stones, which take on a pinkish-violet hue. The fronts of the houses along a street stretching out under a starlit sky are deep blue or violet with a green tree. Here, then, is a night picture without any black in it, nothing but beautiful blue and violet and green, and in those surroundings the lighted square is coloured sulphur yellow and lemon green. I really enjoy doing a painting on the spot at night.'

Letter to Wilhelmina van Gogh

Painted in the same week as his garden scenes, Vincent's picture depicted the exterior of another of the establishments he frequented in Arles, the Grand Café du Forum.

THE OLD MILL
September 1888
Albright-Knox Art Gallery, Buffalo, New York

'I have a study of an old mill painted in broken tones like the oak tree on the rock.'

Letter to Theo

One of the few rural landmarks painted by Vincent that still exist, the old mill sometimes known as Jonquet's Tower rises prominently in the Crau landscape, its fields and the Alpille foothills visible in the background. The road leading to it, now called the rue Mireille, leads from the Mouleyrès, or windmills, quarter of Arles. Windmills, such as those he painted in Montmartre, often feature in Vincent's oeuvre, reminding us of his Dutch origins.

Entrance to the Public Gardens at Arles
September 1888
Phillips Collection, Washington, DC

'What I wanted was to paint the garden in such a way that one would think of Petrarch, the old poet from here (or rather from Avignon) and the new poet living here – Paul Gauguin.'

Letter to Theo

This painting shows the public gardens across from the Yellow House and referred to by him as the 'poet's garden'. It probably dates from this time, although the precise dating of his garden pictures remains confused. The astonishing speed of Vincent's work was exemplified by his paintings of the gardens: in a letter to Theo he told him, 'I wrote to you earlier this morning, after which I carried on with a painting of a garden in the sun. I then brought that one home and went out again with a fresh canvas, and that one, too, is now finished.' He intended them as a homage to Gauguin and as part of the decorations for the house they were to share.

THE YELLOW HOUSE
September 1888
Vincent van Gogh Foundation/National Museum Vincent van Gogh, Amsterdam

'My house here is painted the yellow colour of fresh butter on the outside with glaringly green shutters; it stands in the full sunlight in a square which has a green garden with plane trees, oleanders and acacias. And it is completely whitewashed inside, and the floor is made of red bricks. And over it there is the intensely blue sky. In this I can live and breathe, meditate and paint.'

Letter to Wilhelmina van Gogh

Vincent first slept in the Yellow House on the night of 16-17 September 1888. Gauguin moved in a month later and it was there, two days before Christmas 1888, that Vincent mutilated his ear, resulting in his prolonged stay in Arles hospital. The house was completely destroyed by Allied bombing during the Second World War.

POLLARD WILLOWS WITH SETTING SUN

Autumn 1888

State Museum Kröller-Müller, Otterlo

'Yesterday I painted a sunset.'

Letter to Theo

Vincent's fascination with nature – flowers, trees and even moths – is manifested in much of his work. He had given careful thought to the problems of representing on canvas what he saw in nature, and three years before he moved to Provence had told Theo:

'Of nature I retain a certain sequence and a certain correctness in placing the tones. I study nature so as not to do foolish things, to remain reasonable; however, I don't care so much whether my colour is exactly the same, as long as it looks beautiful on my canvas, as beautiful as it looks in nature . . . suppose I have to paint an autumn landscape, trees with yellow leaves. All right – when I conceive a symphony in yellow, what does it matter if the fundamental colour of yellow is the same as that of the leaves or not? It matters very little.'

THE RED VINEYARD

November 1888

Pushkin Museum, Moscow

'If you had been with us on Sunday, you would have seen a red vineyard, completely red like red wine. In the distance it turned to yellow, and there was also a green sky with the disk of the sun, and the fields, after the rain, violet and here and there glittering yellow, where the setting sun was reflected.'

'I have finished a canvas of a vineyard all purple and yellow, with small blue and violet figures and yellow sunlight.'

Letters to Theo

Vincent had previously painted the same subject, a vineyard not far from Montmajour, as predominantly green, and was now struck by the dramatic colour change. *The Red Vineyard* is known to have been one of his own favourite works, and he sent it for exhibition with the group known as *Les XX* ('The Twenty') in Brussels. The claim that it was the only painting sold in his lifetime (for 400 francs to Anna Boch, painter and sister of Vincent's friend, the poet Eugène Boch) has recently been called into question. When Gauguin painted this identical subject, he incongruously peopled his canvas with Breton women.

JOSEPH ROULIN
April 1889
State Museum Kröller-Müller, Otterlo

'I have just done a portrait of a postman, or rather, two portraits. A Socratic type, none the less so for being somewhat addicted to liquor and having a high colour as a result. His wife has just had a child, and the fellow was aglow with satisfaction . . . . He kept himself too stiff when posing, which is why I painted him twice, the second time at a single sitting. A blue, nearly white background on the white canvas, all the broken tones in the face – yellows, greens, violets, pinks, reds. The uniform Prussian blue, with yellow adornments.'

Letter to Emile Bernard

'Roulin, though he is not quite old enough to be like a father to me, nevertheless has a silent gravity and a tenderness for me . . . he has the strong constitution of the peasant; he always looks well and even jolly.'

Letter to Theo

Joseph-Etienne Roulin, a postal worker at Arles railway station, befriended Vincent who described him as 'a man more interesting than most', painting him and members of his family on several occasions.

THE CRAU WITH PEACH TREES IN BLOOM
April 1889
Courtauld Institute Galleries, London

'I have just come back with two studies of orchards. Here is a crude sketch of them – the big one is a poor landscape with little cottages, blue skyline of the Alpine [Alpille] foothills, sky white and blue. The foreground patches of land surrounded by cane hedges, where small peach trees are in bloom – everything is small there, the gardens, the fields, the orchards, and the trees, even the mountains, as in certain Japanese landscapes, which is the reason why the subject attracted me.'

Letter to Paul Signac

After his self-inflicted injury and mental disturbance, Vincent had recovered sufficiently by April 1889 to work out of doors. His painting of the Crau is one of his first from this period. It is effectively a modified view of his harvest landscape of the previous year. He told Theo, 'how much the Camargue and the Crau, except for the difference in colour and the clearness of the atmosphere, remind me of the old Holland of Ruysdael's time.'

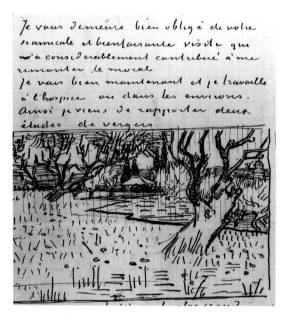

Je vous demeure bien obligé de votre
aimicale et bienfaisante visite qui
m'a considerablement contribué à me
remonter le moral
Je vais bien maintenant et je travaille
à l'hospice ou dans les environs.
Ainsi je viens de rapporter deux
études de vergers.

ORCHARD IN BLOOM WITH VIEW OF ARLES
April 1889
Vincent van Gogh Foundation/National Museum Vincent van Gogh, Amsterdam

'At present I am well, and I work at the sanatorium and its environs. I have just come back with two studies of orchards.'

Letter to Paul Signac

Vincent's *Orchard in Bloom with View of Arles* dates from the same period as his *Crau with Peach Trees in Bloom*. In March, Signac had visited Vincent at the hospital in Arles, finding him, as he wrote to Theo, 'in perfect health, physically and mentally'. The first and larger of the two works he mentioned in his letter to Signac was his painting of *The Crau*, and the second this subject, which he described to him as 'nearly all green with a little lilac and grey – on a rainy day'. He included sketches of both these orchard paintings in his letter.

ORCHARD IN BLOOM WITH POPLARS IN THE FOREGROUND
April 1889

Bayerische Staatsgemäldesammlungen, Neue Pinakothek, Munich

'I have six studies of the spring, two of them big orchards. It is very urgent, because these effects are so short-lived.'

Letter to Theo

Though this painting was not specifically mentioned in his letters of the time, when he was planning to enter several works in the exhibition of *Les XX*, Vincent referred to this painting as '. . . the orchard in bloom, with a row of poplars intersecting the canvas'. It was among the last paintings he executed before transferring to the asylum at Saint-Rémy.

IRISES

May 1889

J. Paul Getty Museum, Malibu

'When you receive the canvases that I have done in the garden, you will see that I am not too melancholy here.'

Letter to Theo

Although irises feature in Vincent's beloved Japanese art, they seldom appeared in Western art before he turned to them. A year earlier, not long after his arrival in Provence, he had painted a view of Arles with irises flanking a field. He had been particularly struck by the flowers' colour and later returned to the motif at Saint-Rémy. After painting them growing in the grounds of the asylum, he was also to paint them cut, in a white vase: among his last works executed in Provence, they represented a symbol of the region's rich colours that had so inspired him. This painting was first shown at the Société des Indépendant's exhibition in September 1889, and in 1987 achieved international fame when it became the most expensive work of art ever sold at auction.

Lilac Bushes
May 1889
Hermitage, Leningrad

'I am working on two paintings – some violet irises and a lilac bush, two motifs taken from the garden.'

Letter to Theo

His *Lilac Bushes* are typical of Vincent's concern to represent nature on canvas; as the novelist Octave Mirbeau wrote in an appreciation within a year of Vincent's death:

'He had absorbed nature into himself; he had forced it to unbend, to mould itself into the shapes of his thoughts, to follow him in his flights, even to submit to his highly characteristic deformations . . . He spares himself no effort, to the benefit of the trees, skies, flowers, fields, which he inflates with the astonishing dream of his being.'

MOUNTAIN LANDSCAPE SEEN ACROSS THE WALLS WITH RISING SUN AND GREEN FIELD

June 1889

State Museum Kröller-Müller, Otterlo

'Quite near here there are some little mountains, grey and blue, and at their foot some very, very green cornfields and pines.'

Letter to Johanna van Gogh

Vincent's *Mountain Landscape*, one of several works painted from his bedroom window at the asylum at Saint-Rémy, includes the enclosing wall, a symbol of his 'imprisonment' there. Previously dated to spring 1890, it has now been reassigned to June 1889, as he is known to have executed little in spring of the following year, during much of which he was too ill to paint.

Starry Night

June 1889

Museum of Modern Art, New York

'Now I really want to paint a starry sky. It often seems to me that the night is still more richly coloured than the day, having hues of the most intense violets, blues and greens. If only you pay attention to it you will see that certain stars are citron-yellow, others have a pink glow, or a green, blue and forget-me-not brilliance. And without my expatiating on this theme it will be clear that putting little white dots on a blue-black surface is not enough.'

Letter to Wilhelmina van Gogh

More than a year previously, Vincent had written to Bernard, telling him, 'A starry sky . . . that is something I should like to try to do', and later asked him, 'When shall I paint my *starry sky*, that picture which preoccupies me continuously?'

WHEATFIELD WITH CYPRESSES
June 1889
National Gallery, London

'The cypresses are always occupying my thoughts, I should like to make something of them like the canvases of the sunflowers, because it astonishes me that they have not yet been done as I see them. It is as beautiful of line and proportion as an Egyptian obelisk. And the green has a quality of such distinction. It is a splash of *black* in a sunny landscape, but it is one of the most interesting black notes, and the most difficult to hit off exactly that I can imagine.'

Letter to Theo

The motif, a wheatfield situated beyond the walls of the asylum, obsessed Vincent, and he returned to it on several occasions. 'The cypress is characteristic of the Provençal landscape,' he told the art critic Albert Aurier, giving him one of his paintings of the subject in gratitude for Aurier's favourable review of his work.

OLIVE ORCHARD
June 1889
State Museum Kröller-Müller, Otterlo

'The olive trees are very characteristic, and I am struggling to catch them. They are old silver, sometimes with more blue in them, sometimes greenish, bronzed, fading white above a soil which is yellow, pink, violet-tinted or orange, to dull red ochre. Very difficult though, very difficult.'

Letter to Theo

Finding no vineyards near Saint-Rémy, Vincent turned his attention to the olive orchards, producing at least two other paintings during the same period and returning to the subject in the autumn of 1889. The earlier versions, of which this is an example, are regarded as more successful than his later series, and they are among his best-known works, many observers reading in these pictures a symbolic connection between their gnarled appearance and Vincent's own 'twisted' mentality.

A Path through the Ravine
December 1889
State Museum Kröller-Müller, Otterlo

'I am working on a large canvas of a *Ravine* . . . two bases of extremely solid rocks, between which there flows a stream; a third mountain blocking the ravine. Such subjects certainly have a fine melancholy, and it's fun to work in such wild places, where one has to wedge the easel in between the stones to prevent the wind from blowing the whole lot over.'

Letter to Emile Bernard

In October Vincent had been allowed to visit the mountainous scenery near Saint-Rémy with a warder from the asylum who was familiar with the locality. The result was a painting of a ravine with two female figures – of which this is effectively a replica – probably painted at the end of the year when the weather was too inclement for him to work outside. Their differences patched up, Gauguin saw the painting and wrote to Vincent with a proposal: 'I should like to exchange with you for anything of mine you choose. The one I mean is a mountainous landscape: two very small travellers seem to be climbing in search of the unknown. It's beautiful and impressive.'

BRANCHES OF AN ALMOND TREE IN BLOSSOM
February 1890
Vincent van Gogh Foundation/National Museum Vincent van Gogh, Amsterdam

'I started right away to make a picture for him, to hang in their bedroom, big branches of white almond blossom against a blue sky.'

Letter to Wilhelmina van Gogh

'. . . a day or two ago I started painting a picture for her [Jo] of a blue sky full of branches full of blossoms standing out against it.'

Letter to Theo

Believed to have been painted indoors from a cut branch rather than from a growing tree, this painting was important to Vincent as a symbol of new life, produced as a present for Theo and Jo (his wife Johanna) to mark the birth of their child – a boy named after Vincent. Soon after painting it he suffered a major attack and did not write to Theo again for two months. When he resumed writing, he told him, 'My work was going well, the last canvas of branches in blossom – you will see that it was perhaps the best, most patiently worked thing I had done, painted with calm and with a greater firmness of touch. And the next day, down like a brute.'

The following month, Vincent moved to Auvers-sur-Oise, where he was to soon end his life.

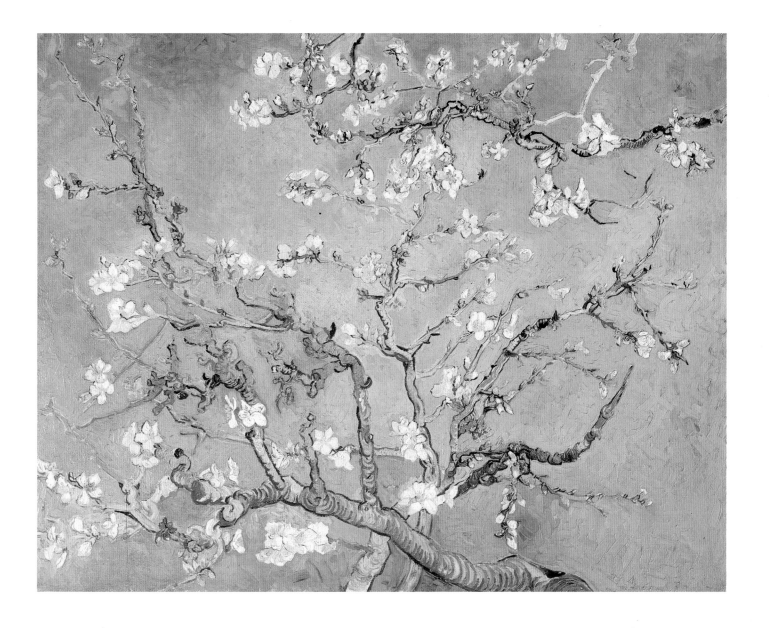

First published in Great Britain in 1994 by
PAVILION BOOKS LIMITED
London House, Great Eastern Wharf, Parkgate Road
London SW11 4NQ

This edition published in 1998 by
Tiger Books International PLC, Twickenham, U.K.

Designed by Bernard Higton
Picture research by Kate Russell-Cobb

A CIP catalogue record for this book is available from
the British Library.

ISBN 1 85501 985 X

2 4 6 8 10 9 7 5 3 1

Printed in China by Sun Fung Offset Binding Co.
Produced in association with The Hanway Press Ltd., London

Picture credits
All plates are from the sources shown in the captions unless
otherwise indicated below.

Additional picture sources: Front cover (*Harvest Landscape,*
1888), page 1 (*Self-portrait with Straw Hat and Pipe,* 1888), 4,
6, 9 right, 10, 20, 34, 42, 44, 56 Vincent van Gogh
Foundation/National Museum Vincent van Gogh,
Amsterdam; 2 (*The Sower,* 1888), 8 left, 11 (*Mountain
Landscape Seen Across the Walls,* 1890) State Museum
Kröller-Müller, Otterlo; 5 Map of van Gogh's Provence by
David Atkinson; 7, 23 Musée d'Orsay/Photos © RMN; 8
centre Pushkin Museum, Moscow/Scala; 8 bottom right, 18
Oskar Reinhart Foundation, Winterthur; 9 left Courtauld
Institute Galleries, London; 25 left, 47 Artothek; 33
Photographie Giraudon; 39, 51 Scala; 49 Sotheby's; Back
cover (*Starry Night,* 1889), Museum of Modern Art, New
York. Acquired through the Lillie P. Bliss Bequest.